AUDIO ACCESS INCLUDED
Recorded Piano Accompaniments Online

CLARINET IN B-FLAT & PIANO

THE SOUND OF MUSIC
FOR CLASSICAL PLAYERS

To access recorded piano accompaniments online, visit:
www.halleonard.com/mylibrary

Enter Code
4272-2302-8567-0344

ISBN: 978-1-5400-3752-7

THE RODGERS &
HAMMERSTEIN
ORGANIZATION

R&H

A CONCORD COMPANY

EXCLUSIVELY DISTRIBUTED BY

HAL•LEONARD®

For all works contained herein:
Unauthorized copying, arranging, adapting, recording, Internet posting, public performance,
or other distribution of the music in this publication is an infringement of copyright.
Infringers are liable under the law.

Visit Hal Leonard Online at
www.halleonard.com

Contact Us:
Hal Leonard
7777 West Bluemound Road
Milwaukee, WI 53213
Email: info@halleonard.com

In Europe contact:
Hal Leonard Europe Limited
Distribution Centre, Newmarket Road
Bury St Edmunds, Suffolk, IP33 3YB
Email: info@halleonardeurope.com

In Australia contact:
Hal Leonard Australia Pty. Ltd.
4 Lentara Court
Cheltenham, Victoria, 3192 Australia
Email: info@halleonard.com.au

HOW TO USE HAL LEONARD ONLINE AUDIO

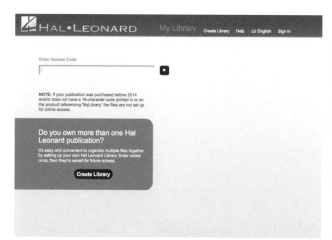

Because of the changing use of media, and the fact that fewer people are using CDs, we have made a shift to companion audio accessible online. In many cases, rather than a book with CD, we now have a book with an access code for online audio, including performances, accompaniments or diction lessons. Each copy of each book has a unique access code. We call this Hal Leonard created system "My Library." It's simple to use.

Go to www.halleonard.com/mylibrary and enter the unique access code found on page one of a relevant book/audio package.

The audio tracks can be streamed or downloaded. If you download the tracks on your computer, you can add the files to a CD or to your digital music library, and use them anywhere without being online. See below for comments about Apple and Android mobile devices.

There are some great benefits to the My Library system. *Playback+* is exclusive to Hal Leonard, and when connected to the Internet with this multi-functional audio player you can:

• Change tempo without changing pitch
• Transpose to any key

Optionally, you can create a My Library account, and store all the companion audio you have purchased there. Access your account online at any time, from any device, by logging into your account at www.halleonard.com/mylibrary. Technical help may be found at www.halleonard.com/mylibrary/help/

Apple/iOS

Question: On my iPad and iPhone, the Download links just open another browser tab and play the track. How come this doesn't really download?

Answer: The Safari iOS browser will not allow you to download audio files directly in iTunes or other apps. There are several ways to work around this:

• You can download normally on your desktop computer, saving the files to iTunes. Then, you can sync your iOS device directly to your computer, or sync your iTunes content using an iCloud account.
• There are many third-party apps which allow you to download files from websites into the app's own file manager for easy retrieval and playback.

Android

Files are always downloaded to the same location, which is a folder usually called "Downloads" (this may vary slightly depending on what browser is used (Chrome, Firefox, etc)). Chrome uses a system app called "Downloads" where files can be accessed at any time. Firefox and some other browsers store downloaded files within a "Downloads" folder in the browser itself.

Recently-downloaded files can be accessed from the Notification bar; swiping down will show the downloaded files as a new "card", which you tap on to open. Opening a file depends on what apps are installed on the Android device. Audio files are opened in the device's default audio app. If a file type does not have a default app assigned to it, the Android system alerts the user.

CONTENTS

Pianist on the recordings: [1]Brendan Fox, [2]Ruben Piirainen

The price of this publication includes access to companion recorded piano accompaniments online,

for download or streaming, using the unique code found on the title page.

Visit www.halleonard.com/mylibrary and enter the access code.

Climb Ev'ry Mountain

Lyrics by Oscar Hammerstein II
Music by Richard Rodgers

Copyright © 1959 Williamson Music Company c/o Concord Music Publishing
Copyright Renewed
This arrangement Copyright © 2019 Williamson Music Company c/o Concord Music Publishing
All Rights Reserved   Used by Permission

Do-Re-Mi

Lyrics by Oscar Hammerstein II
Music by Richard Rodgers

Copyright © 1959 Williamson Music Company c/o Concord Music Publishing
Copyright Renewed
This arrangement Copyright © 2019 Williamson Music Company c/o Concord Music Publishing
All Rights Reserved   Used by Permission

Tempo di Marcia

Edelweiss

Lyrics by Oscar Hammerstein II
Music by Richard Rodgers

Copyright © 1959 Williamson Music Company c/o Concord Music Publishing
Copyright Renewed
This arrangement Copyright © 2019 Williamson Music Company c/o Concord Music Publishing
All Rights Reserved   Used by Permission

The Lonely Goatherd

Lyrics by Oscar Hammerstein II
Music by Richard Rodgers

Copyright © 1959 Williamson Music Company c/o Concord Music Publishing
Copyright Renewed
This arrangement Copyright © 2019 Williamson Music Company c/o Concord Music Publishing
All Rights Reserved   Used by Permission

I Have Confidence

Lyrics and Music by
Richard Rodgers

Copyright © 1965 Williamson Music Company c/o Concord Music Publishing
Copyright Renewed
This arrangement Copyright © 2019 Williamson Music Company c/o Concord Music Publishing
All Rights Reserved   Used by Permission

THE SOUND OF MUSIC
FOR CLASSICAL PLAYERS

To access recorded piano accompaniments online, visit:
www.halleonard.com/mylibrary

Enter Code
5662-6412-8049-7620

ISBN: 978-1-5400-3752-7

**THE RODGERS &
HAMMERSTEIN
ORGANIZATION**

R&H

A CONCORD COMPANY

EXCLUSIVELY DISTRIBUTED BY

HAL•LEONARD®

For all works contained herein:
Unauthorized copying, arranging, adapting, recording, Internet posting, public performance,
or other distribution of the music in this publication is an infringement of copyright.
Infringers are liable under the law.

Visit Hal Leonard Online at
www.halleonard.com

Contact Us:
Hal Leonard
7777 West Bluemound Road
Milwaukee, WI 53213
Email: info@halleonard.com

In Europe contact:
Hal Leonard Europe Limited
Distribution Centre, Newmarket Road
Bury St Edmunds, Suffolk, IP33 3YB
Email: info@halleonardeurope.com

In Australia contact:
Hal Leonard Australia Pty. Ltd.
4 Lentara Court
Cheltenham, Victoria, 3192 Australia
Email: info@halleonard.com.au

HOW TO USE HAL LEONARD ONLINE AUDIO

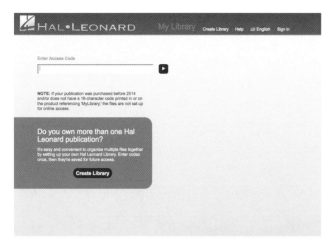

Because of the changing use of media, and the fact that fewer people are using CDs, we have made a shift to companion audio accessible online. In many cases, rather than a book with CD, we now have a book with an access code for online audio, including performances, accompaniments or diction lessons. Each copy of each book has a unique access code. We call this Hal Leonard created system "My Library." It's simple to use.

Go to www.halleonard.com/mylibrary and enter the unique access code found on page one of a relevant book/audio package.

The audio tracks can be streamed or downloaded. If you download the tracks on your computer, you can add the files to a CD or to your digital music library, and use them anywhere without being online. See below for comments about Apple and Android mobile devices.

There are some great benefits to the My Library system. *Playback+* is exclusive to Hal Leonard, and when connected to the Internet with this multi-functional audio player you can:

• Change tempo without changing pitch
• Transpose to any key

Optionally, you can create a My Library account, and store all the companion audio you have purchased there. Access your account online at any time, from any device, by logging into your account at www.halleonard.com/mylibrary. Technical help may be found at www.halleonard.com/mylibrary/help/

Apple/iOS

Question: On my iPad and iPhone, the Download links just open another browser tab and play the track. How come this doesn't really download?

Answer: The Safari iOS browser will not allow you to download audio files directly in iTunes or other apps. There are several ways to work around this:

• You can download normally on your desktop computer, saving the files to iTunes. Then, you can sync your iOS device directly to your computer, or sync your iTunes content using an iCloud account.

• There are many third-party apps which allow you to download files from websites into the app's own file manager for easy retrieval and playback.

Android

Files are always downloaded to the same location, which is a folder usually called "Downloads" (this may vary slightly depending on what browser is used (Chrome, Firefox, etc)). Chrome uses a system app called "Downloads" where files can be accessed at any time. Firefox and some other browsers store downloaded files within a "Downloads" folder in the browser itself.

Recently-downloaded files can be accessed from the Notification bar; swiping down will show the downloaded files as a new "card", which you tap on to open. Opening a file depends on what apps are installed on the Android device. Audio files are opened in the device's default audio app. If a file type does not have a default app assigned to it, the Android system alerts the user.

CONTENTS

Pianists on the recordings: [1]Brendan Fox, [2]Ruben Piirainen

The price of this publication includes access to companion recorded piano accompaniments online,

for download or streaming, using the unique code found on the title page.

Visit www.halleonard.com/mylibrary and enter the access code.

4

Climb Ev'ry Mountain

Lyrics by Oscar Hammerstein II
Music by Richard Rodgers

Copyright © 1959 Williamson Music Company c/o Concord Music Publishing
Copyright Renewed
This arrangement Copyright © 2019 Williamson Music Company c/o Concord Music Publishing
All Rights Reserved   Used by Permission

5

Edelweiss

Lyrics by Oscar Hammerstein II
Music by Richard Rodgers

Copyright © 1959 Williamson Music Company c/o Concord Music Publishing
Copyright Renewed
This arrangement Copyright © 2019 Williamson Music Company c/o Concord Music Publishing
All Rights Reserved   Used by Permission

6

Do-Re-Mi

Lyrics by Oscar Hammerstein II
Music by Richard Rodgers

Allegretto

Copyright © 1959 Williamson Music Company c/o Concord Music Publishing
Copyright Renewed
This arrangement Copyright © 2019 Williamson Music Company c/o Concord Music Publishing
All Rights Reserved   Used by Permission

I Have Confidence

Lyrics and Music by
Richard Rodgers

Copyright © 1965 Williamson Music Company c/o Concord Music Publishing
Copyright Renewed
This arrangement Copyright © 2019 Williamson Music Company c/o Concord Music Publishing
All Rights Reserved   Used by Permission

The Lonely Goatherd

Lyrics by Oscar Hammerstein II
Music by Richard Rodgers

Copyright © 1959 Williamson Music Company c/o Concord Music Publishing
Copyright Renewed
This arrangement Copyright © 2019 Williamson Music Company c/o Concord Music Publishing
All Rights Reserved   Used by Permission

Maria

Lyrics by Oscar Hammerstein II
Music by Richard Rodgers

Copyright © 1959 Williamson Music Company c/o Concord Music Publishing
Copyright Renewed
This arrangement Copyright © 2019 Williamson Music Company c/o Concord Music Publishing
All Rights Reserved   Used by Permission

My Favorite Things

Lyrics by Oscar Hammerstein II
Music by Richard Rodgers

Copyright © 1959 Williamson Music Company c/o Concord Music Publishing
Copyright Renewed
This arrangement Copyright © 2019 Williamson Music Company c/o Concord Music Publishing
All Rights Reserved   Used by Permission

Sixteen Going on Seventeen

Lyrics by Oscar Hammerstein II
Music by Richard Rodgers

Copyright © 1959 Williamson Music Company c/o Concord Music Publishing
Copyright Renewed
This arrangement Copyright © 2019 Williamson Music Company c/o Concord Music Publishing
All Rights Reserved   Used by Permission

Ländler

By Richard Rodgers

Copyright © 1959 Williamson Music Company c/o Concord Music Publishing
Copyright Renewed
This arrangement Copyright © 2019 Williamson Music Company c/o Concord Music Publishing
All Rights Reserved   Used by Permission

Something Good

Lyrics and Music by
Richard Rodgers

Copyright © 1965 Williamson Music Company c/o Concord Music Publishing
Copyright Renewed
This arrangement Copyright © 2019 Williamson Music Company c/o Concord Music Publishing
All Rights Reserved   Used by Permission

The Sound of Music

Lyrics by Oscar Hammerstein II
Music by Richard Rodgers

Allegretto animato   Tranquillo

Con espressione

Copyright © 1959 Williamson Music Company c/o Concord Music Publishing
Copyright Renewed
This arrangement Copyright © 2019 Williamson Music Company c/o Concord Music Publishing
All Rights Reserved   Used by Permission

Wedding Processional

Lyrics by Oscar Hammerstein II
Music by Richard Rodgers

Copyright © 1959 Williamson Music Company c/o Concord Music Publishing
Copyright Renewed
This arrangement Copyright © 2019 Williamson Music Company c/o Concord Music Publishing
All Rights Reserved   Used by Permission

Ländler

By Richard Rodgers

Copyright © 1959 Williamson Music Company c/o Concord Music Publishing
Copyright Renewed
This arrangement Copyright © 2019 Williamson Music Company c/o Concord Music Publishing
All Rights Reserved   Used by Permission

Maria

Lyrics by Oscar Hammerstein II
Music by Richard Rodgers

Copyright © 1959 Williamson Music Company c/o Concord Music Publishing
Copyright Renewed
This arrangement Copyright © 2019 Williamson Music Company c/o Concord Music Publishing
All Rights Reserved   Used by Permission

34

Sixteen Going on Seventeen

Lyrics by Oscar Hammerstein II
Music by Richard Rodgers

Copyright © 1959 Williamson Music Company c/o Concord Music Publishing
Copyright Renewed
This arrangement Copyright © 2019 Williamson Music Company c/o Concord Music Publishing
All Rights Reserved   Used by Permission

Something Good

Lyrics and Music by
Richard Rodgers

Copyright © 1965 Williamson Music Company c/o Concord Music Publishing
Copyright Renewed
This arrangement Copyright © 2019 Williamson Music Company c/o Concord Music Publishing
All Rights Reserved   Used by Permission

The Sound of Music

Lyrics by Oscar Hammerstein II
Music by Richard Rodgers

Copyright © 1959 Williamson Music Company c/o Concord Music Publishing
Copyright Renewed
This arrangement Copyright © 2019 Williamson Music Company c/o Concord Music Publishing
All Rights Reserved   Used by Permission

Con espressione

Wedding Processional

Lyrics by Oscar Hammerstein II
Music by Richard Rodgers

Copyright © 1959 Williamson Music Company c/o Concord Music Publishing
Copyright Renewed
This arrangement Copyright © 2019 Williamson Music Company c/o Concord Music Publishing
All Rights Reserved   Used by Permission

My Favorite Things

Lyrics by Oscar Hammerstein II
Music by Richard Rodgers

Copyright © 1959 Williamson Music Company c/o Concord Music Publishing
Copyright Renewed
This arrangement Copyright © 2019 Williamson Music Company c/o Concord Music Publishing
All Rights Reserved   Used by Permission